BERLIN IN THE COLD WAR
1959 to 1966

Allan Hailstone

AMBERLEY

First published 2017

Amberley Publishing
The Hill, Stroud
Gloucestershire, GL5 4EP

www.amberley-books.com

Copyright © Allan Hailstone, 2017

The right of Allan Hailstone to be identified as the
Author of this work has been asserted in accordance
with the Copyrights, Designs and Patents Act 1988.

ISBN 978 1 4456 7290 8 (print)
ISBN 978 1 4456 7291 5 (ebook)

British Library Cataloguing in Publication Data.
A catalogue record for this book is available from
the British Library.

Typeset in 10pt on 13pt Celeste.
Typesetting by Amberley Publishing.
Printed in the UK.

About This Book

Berlin is a skeleton which aches in the cold: it is my own skeleton aching. I feel in my bones the sharp ache of the frost in the girders of the overhead railway, in the ironwork of balconies, in bridges ...
Christopher Isherwood, *A Berlin Diary, 1932–33*

It was probably around 1956 when I took a break from school homework and paid my weekly visit to Coventry library. I picked up a slim volume with black covers entitled *Berlin*; it was an unappealing effort, the very antithesis of what a good guidebook should be. However, as I perused its pages, I was fascinated by the grainy black and white pictures of the city as it then was. I had already spent time pursuing my hobby of photographing the streets of cities in Britain and Europe, but here was something I felt I wanted to see and capture for myself: not the charm of a Paris or Rome – which I had in any case by that time already seen and photographed – but a city like nowhere else, with palpable atmosphere and decay, arising from the ashes of war, and, even better, locked behind the Iron Curtain, divided into sectors with each having their own identity, and even, in the case of the Russian Sector, its own currency.

The following year I moved to university in London, and soon made plans to visit. Brussels and its Expo 58 was too much of an attraction in 1958, which I visited twice, but early in 1959 I travelled by ferry and train to Hanover, one of the three cities from which one could fly to West Berlin using the permitted air corridors, and then on by air, landing in West Berlin one evening in March 1959.

West Berlin had an unusual and attractive atmosphere, a sort of openness. It is difficult to expand on this. The famous *Berliner Luft* ('Berlin air') refers not only to the air quality; it also relates to the way the city feels. It is something that is largely absent in, say, London.

East Berlin was a different matter entirely. Entering from the Tiergarten via the classic route through the Brandenburg Gate, the transition was palpable. Firstly, the famous dramatic sign that one was leaving West Berlin '*jetzt*' ('here'), about a hundred metres in front of the impressive stone structure itself. Contrary to popular opinion, the border was at that point, not at the Brandenburg Gate itself. The red flag in front of the Gate confirmed that the East Germans claimed the entire edifice as their possession. Further along, past the Gate, lay the beginning of Unter den Linden – in earlier days, Berlin's principal thoroughfare.

First impressions are always said to be important, and one that has been remarked on by many observers, but which is impossible to convey, is the distinctive smell of East Berlin. It was not a particularly unpleasant odour, but it always materialised, at whatever locality one crossed to the East. Theories have been raised as to the cause, from vehicle exhausts to the universally used 'state' cleaning fluid. The next oddity was the silence and the absence of traffic (*see the shot of Unter den Linden on page 30*). Occasionally a yellow bus could be seen, with its distinctive front *schnauze* (snout), unlike those in West Berlin. Cars were somewhat of a rarity. The rubble of bombed buildings still lay in the streets, fifteen years after the war.

One of the principal contrasts with West Berlin was the colour. Everything was in pastel shades. After West Berlin, with its multi-coloured surroundings and advertisements of every hue, the difference was striking. Nowhere could be seen anything resembling 'Coca-Cola red'. Certainly, a major difference between the West and countries behind the Iron Curtain was the absence of Coca-Cola and Western advertising itself. Even the communist banners festooning the buildings were in a dull red colour. There was a semblance of Western advertising, for example for East German Persil and Eastern Bloc airlines, or for communist magazines, but one yearned to see something striking in garish colours.

At the end of Unter den Linden was Marx-Engels-Platz, the East German answer to Red Square in Moscow, the location of May Day parades. Here one was truly enveloped in the communist ideology, with the seats for spectators and an enormous anti-Western slogan above. Further on, past the Red Town Hall, the showpiece boulevard of Stalinallee (as it was named in 1959) was a classic example of Soviet 'Wedding Cake' architecture. However, closer inspection revealed that it was falling to pieces in many places.

There was one big positive aspect in visiting the East. In West Berlin it was possible to exchange currency in Bureaux de Change at rates providing up to eight East Marks (resembling 'toy money') to one West Mark, and one was not controlled when crossing over. This resulted in goods and services being obtainable ridiculously cheaply. However, much was in short supply in the East. Bananas, for example, were almost unobtainable in the East, and a street where the border ran down the centre of the street had well-stocked greengrocers on one side, and virtually nothing on display on the other.

On returning to West Berlin on foot, the boundary notices in East Berlin had an appearance somewhat different from those in the West when moving in the opposite direction. They simply stated that at so many metres past the board one would be leaving the 'democratic sector' (*see example on page 19*). Alternatively, one could travel by

4

U-Bahn through, for example, Potsdamer Platz. On arrival of the train at the station, an announcement would be made twice: '*Letzte Bahnhof im demokratischen Sektor*' ('Last station in the democratic sector'). The train would move off, the lights would go out for about ten seconds, and then in a minute or so one was in a different world – a U-Bahn station with brightly coloured advertisements.

On returning to England, it was no small disappointment to find that a fault on my camera had rendered my photographic efforts considerably out of focus, and only one of the March 1959 trip is in this book (*see page 10*). I immediately resolved to return to Berlin, which I did, accompanied by a university friend, in September of that year, when I tried to duplicate many of the shots I had taken in March. A further visit in July 1960 provided further opportunities to photograph the city, without there being any indication of the momentous events to follow the following year. This was my last visit before the Berlin Wall was built, and I returned to Berlin in August 1962.

The Berlin of 1962 was a very different place from the one I had left two years earlier. There was to be no gentle ambling across a street from one side of the Iron Curtain to the other. Foreigners were made to cross either at Checkpoint Charlie, or by train via Friedrichstrasse Station, also with the requirement of exchanging a minimum amount of currency at a rate of 1:1. The overall atmosphere of both West and East Berlin was similar to before 1961, but the citizens of the East were kept behind a control zone near the border, whereas in the West anyone could approach the Wall and even look over it from observation platforms.

The East German regime maintained the charade that the Wall was built to keep fascist invaders from infiltrating the East, but this pretence was fatuous; to the outside world it was obvious that the increasing number of people fleeing to the West was unsustainable, and some form of physical barrier had become necessary. At first, this consisted simply of barbed wire across the streets; soon this was augmented with crude concrete blocks. The regime overlooked some simple escape routes such as in Bernauer Strasse (*see page 66*), where the apartments on the northern side were in East Berlin, with the adjacent pavement in West Berlin. The inhabitants could simply lower themselves out from the windows to 'freedom'. This was quickly spotted, and the citizens were moved out and the windows bricked up.

In later years the Wall was made higher, and its crude appearance improved (*see the photographs in 1964*). Still later, a more sophisticated and much higher barrier was erected, topped by a greased pole replacing the barbed wire.

It was inadvisable to photograph the border area from the Eastern side, as this was heavily patrolled and everyone approaching it was watched. An exception was near the Brandenburg Gate (*see page 90*), which was maintained as a symbol of Berlin, and from which area the Wall could only just be spotted in the distance on the far side of the monument.

East Berlin was no longer the place for bargain purchases, formerly possible owing to the market rate for East Marks. Although it was still possible to buy East Marks cheaply in the West, it was highly inadvisable to take them into the East, as one was liable to be searched on entry. Export of East Marks was also prohibited. I was sent back to exchange a few pfennigs at Friedrichstrasse on one occasion, although I doubt it would have damaged the East German economy if I had taken them back to the West.

At Friedrichstrasse station visitors from the West passed through a Customs Hall, at which there were many tearful goodbyes. After German reunification this hall became a nightclub known as Tränenpalast (The Palace of Tears).

Berlin, now reunited, has again become one city, and a centre of many cultures. Visitors trace the course of the former Wall, following a path of bricks set into the road across the city. The rebuilt Potsdamer Platz is unrecognisable from its immediate post-war appearance or its glory in pre-war days. The scene in the Wim Wenders movie *Wings of Desire* where the old man trudges through Potsdamer Platz unable to comprehend his surroundings will still be understood by a dwindling few. However, modern visitors will not begin to appreciate the flavour of the way the city felt when divided. I hope that this book will help to provide a taste of those days.

Berlin: A Brief History

Berlin was founded in about the thirteenth century around the banks of the Spree and Havel rivers. It grew in size, becoming the capital of Prussia in 1701, and in 1871 the capital of the German Empire. After its role in both World Wars and the defeat of Germany in the Second World War, the occupying powers agreed at the 1945 Potsdam Conference that Germany should be temporarily divided into three, later four, zones. Berlin, which lay within the Soviet Zone, was similarly divided into four sectors: British, French, American and Soviet, the latter being the largest.

As the Cold War intensified, the de facto situation was that the British, French and American sectors came to be known as West Berlin, and the Soviet sector East Berlin. The corresponding areas of Germany were termed West Germany and East Germany.

In 1948, when the Western Powers introduced currency reform into West Berlin, the Soviets imposed a blockade on the access routes to the city, which lay entirely within the Soviet Zone of Germany. The Allied Powers countered this with an airlift to supply the city, which lasted almost a year. In 1949 the Western and Soviet zones were proclaimed by the respective powers as the Federal Republic of Germany, capital Bonn, and the German Democratic Republic, capital Berlin.

As communism took hold in East Germany, the citizens became progressively more dissatisfied, resulting in an uprising in June 1953. Refugees began to flee in increasing numbers to the West, taking advantage of the fact that in Berlin one could walk across the street into the West without any controls and then fly out to West Germany using three 'air corridors', in which aircraft registered in the UK, France or the US were permitted to operate. This outflow reached epidemic proportions by August 1961, and on the 13th of that month the East Germans sealed the border between East and West Berlin with barbed wire, and shortly afterwards with crude concrete blocks to form a wall.

The Berlin Wall, as it came to be known, was fortified further in later years, and a number of stand-offs between East and West occurred, with tanks at Checkpoint Charlie, one of the main crossing points, on one notable occasion. A number of these control points allowed most Westerners to pass between West and East, subject to various conditions.

A Four-Power Agreement in 1971 attempted to regularise relationships between East and West, but with the relaxation of communism under Glasnost and increased transparency in the Soviet Union, by 1989 it was evident that the situation needed to change. The first cracks began to appear on 9 November of that year, when citizens pulled down a section of the Wall near the Brandenburg Gate. Shortly after this, free movement between East and West Berlin became the norm. Within a year, on 3 October 1990, Germany was reunified as the Federal Republic of Germany, with Berlin again the capital.

The city, arguably the foremost centre of conflict in the twentieth century, is now a major tourist centre, and a cultural capital for music, theatre and cinema. Whichever events shape its future, it will surely remain a focus of world attention, and, for many, an unchanging place that ties them emotionally. As Berliners say: '*Berlin bleibt doch Berlin*' ('Berlin always remains Berlin').

Acknowledgements

I am most grateful to Connor Stait of Amberley Publishing, without whose interest in the subject of Berlin in the Cold War this book would not have been possible; to Sheila Beckett, who accompanied me to Berlin and encouraged me over several years to pursue the idea of this book; to others who were with me in Berlin and who enabled me to see the city through new eyes and as if for the first time: my late father, Fred (who bought me the camera), my wife Judith, Barry Daniells, Michael Browne, Chris and Missi Eimer; also their daughter Nicola, who visited the city and decided to live there rather than in London.

Before The Wall

The Junction of the Communist Giants, 24 March 1959
'If you are looking for John-Foster-Dulles-Allee, madam, you won't find it around here.' This is the only photograph in this book from my first visit to Berlin in March 1959, when I found on my return that my camera had developed a focusing fault. I am including it because I do not feel that the fault detracts from the image; in fact, it may arguably be said to enhance the feel of this desolate half of this city. I returned to Berlin later in the year to re-photograph many of the scenes I captured in March.

Kongresshalle, West Berlin, 8 September 1959
Kongresshalle (Congress Hall), in the Tiergarten, was built a year or two before I took this photograph. Its unusual design gave rise to the Berliners' nickname of the 'pregnant oyster'. In 1980 the building collapsed and was rebuilt, opening in 1987. I used to visit the restaurant in the old building and was amazed to find the new one to be identical, even down to the interior decoration. The building is now known as Haus der Kulturen der Welt (House of the World's Cultures). The nearby road John-Foster-Dulles-Allee commemorates the US Secretary of State who died in May 1959. No doubt this road had only been recently renamed.

At the Soviet War Memorial, West Berlin, 8 September 1959

These two Soviet soldiers were guarding their War Memorial in the Tiergarten in West Berlin. (*See page 29 for further background information*). The main inscription on the memorial reads, in translation, 'Eternal glory to heroes who fell in battle with the German fascist invaders for the freedom and independence of the Soviet Union.'

Brandenburger Tor, 8 September 1959

Built around 1790, Brandenburger Tor (the Brandenburg Gate) symbolised the division of Berlin. Contrary to common belief, the frontier lay not at the Gate, but several metres nearer the camera, and the Tor itself was entirely on East Berlin territory. The notice on the left warns that the border lies 40 metres further on, and the smaller notice on the right states that the border is '*jetzt*' (here, at this point). In fact, it would have been a fraction beyond, as the notice must have stood on Western territory. The Berlin Wall was later built as a large semi-circular arc between the Tor and the camera position.

Alexanderplatz, East Berlin, 8 September 1959

Alexanderplatz was arguably, together with Unter den Linden and Stalinallee, the focal point of activity of East Berlin. An enormously depressing place, 'Alex', as it is still known, possessed several cafes serving sub-standard food, together with HO and KONSUM stores reminiscent of wartime co-operative shops in the UK. The contrast with West Berlin's thriving activity was startling. This area now includes Fernsehturm (the television tower) and much else, but still retains some of the atmosphere of the communist era.

East Berlin, 8 September 1959

I came upon this scene on a building site near Alexanderplatz. Although the role of men and women has become more normalised since then, I was startled to see this woman performing hard manual labour tasks. The role of both sexes as manual workers has of course always been stressed in communist countries.

In a restaurant, East Berlin, 8 September 1959

I took this shot in a restaurant, which I remember as being somewhat near Alexanderplatz. Restaurants in East Berlin were depressing places, and much food was unobtainable. What was available on the limited menu tended to be duplicated from one eating place to another; seating was uncomfortable and the general atmosphere was that of a works canteen. However, because of the highly favourable exchange rate obtainable for East Marks in West Berlin, the food was very inexpensive.

Relaxing on Stalinallee, East Berlin, 8 September 1959

This was one of the more pleasant ways in which it was possible to relax outdoors in East Berlin. As mentioned elsewhere, the food available was limited but relatively inexpensive, and the comforts of the restaurant somewhat austere; the musical accompaniment would have been conservative in nature, usually classical music. Jazz and popular music were frowned upon, yet often enjoyed behind closed doors.

Stalinallee, East Berlin, 8 September 1959
These two photographs show further examples of the propaganda boards that were commonplace in the streets of East Berlin (*see also page 16*). The cartoon depictions were often accompanied by two-line poetical quips, as seen here. The dog in the rocket refers to Laika, the Soviet dog that was sent into space on Sputnik 2 in November 1957. The circumstances of the dog's death on the flight were not revealed until many years later.

Unter den Linden and Reichstag, 9 September 1959
This is an example of how the East German Government had left buildings as ruins fourteen years after the end of the Second World War, although demolition had begun since my visit earlier in the year and was completed in 1960. From my posting on the Flickr photographic website, this building has been variously identified as the Friedlander-Fuld building and the headquarters of the Generalinspecteur für das Strassenwesen of the Deutsches Reich. It stood at the very western end of Unter den Linden on Pariser Platz, next to the sector border. The Reichstag building, which was entirely in West Berlin, can be seen in the background undergoing renovation.

Unter den Linden, East Berlin, 9 September 1959
This view looks eastwards at the end of Unter den Linden, which is furthest from Brandenburger Tor. Buildings seen here include the Neue Wache (New Guardhouse) behind the coach and the Zeughaus (Military Museum), above which protrudes the top of Berlin Cathedral; at the end of Unter den Linden is Marx-Engels-Platz, with stands for spectators, and in the distance is the Rotes Rathaus (the Red Town Hall).

Propaganda posters at the Opera House, East Berlin, 9 September 1959
Propaganda posters such as these were commonplace on the streets in the East. I photographed these outside the Opera House (Deutsche Oper) at the eastern end of Unter den Linden. The one nearest to the camera depicts Willy Brandt (1913–92, at the time the mayor of West Berlin) as a lapel decoration on the suit of Konrad Adenauer (1876–1967, then the Chairman of the centre-right Christlich Demokratische Union and the Chancellor of West Germany). The legend reads: '*Brandt, die Perle der C.D.U.*' (Brandt, the pearl of the CDU). Willy Brandt subsequently became the Chancellor of West Germany in 1969.

Marx-Engels-Platz, East Berlin, 9 September 1959
Marx-Engels-Platz was the East German answer to Red Square in Moscow. Named in 1951 after Karl Marx and Friedrich Engels, the authors of *The Communist Manifesto*, it was the location for the communist May Day and other rallies. At the far end are stands erected for spectators; beyond is the Rotes Rathaus (Red Town Hall). After the reunification of Germany the square was renamed Schlossplatz in 1994, and became a car park.

East Berlin, 9 September 1959
It is unlikely that statues such as these
would have been encountered outside
the communist world. These stood near
Alexanderplatz as a hymn to manual
labour by both sexes, struggling to build
their democratic republic, including,
two years later, the Berlin Wall.
The male version still stood here when
I visited in 2009.

Berliner Dom and Marx-Engels-Platz, East Berlin, 9 September 1959
This shot of the Berliner Dom (*Berlin Cathedral; see also page 31*) shows additionally the stands for spectators in Marx-Engels-Platz. The board on the right was used to exhibit large propaganda banners.

Near Alexanderplatz, East Berlin, 9 September 1959
One of the noticeable differences between advertising pitches in West and East Berlin was that advertisements for Coca-Cola, ubiquitous in the West, were completely absent in the East. Advertising in the East was somewhat more low-key, and would usually be in the form of anti-Western slogans, or for cinemas and cultural activities, or extolling the positive aspects of manual labour. It was very common to see political slogans festooning the entire lengths of public buildings, buses and trams.

Border controls, Potsdamer Platz, Berlin,
9 September 1959
The People's Police are here making random checks
on passengers entering Potsdamer Platz S-Bahn
station in East Berlin, a few steps from the border
with West Berlin. I took this photograph while
standing just inside West Berlin. My school friend,
who moved one more step into the East to get a
better shot, was apprehended and the film from his
camera exposed to the light.

Stresemannstrasse, 9 September 1959
This juxtaposition of border crossing signs was often seen at the boundary between West and
East Berlin. The nearer sign is obviously a DDR (East German) sign standing on DDR territory,
since it refers to the end of the 'democratic' (East) sector being 22 metres further on, whereas
the sign on the right-hand side lies in West Berlin and advises that one is leaving the American
sector beyond this point. This view along Stresemannstrasse is from the edge of Potsdamer
Platz; the border crossed this street several times, sometimes with the buildings in West Berlin
and the immediately adjoining pavement in the East.

Cafe on the border, 9 September 1959
This was a convenient cafe on Potsdamer Platz where one could have a drink or a snack and watch the comings and goings between West and East Berlin. It was situated a few steps inside West Berlin, and a little further down to the left the white railings actually formed the border. The man is reading *Neues Deutschland*, the East German newspaper. Whether a cafe patron in East Berlin reading a Western newspaper would be tolerated is another matter.

Electric news board, Potsdamer Platz, West Berlin, 9 September 1959
This structure in Potsdamer Platz beamed news from 1950 to 1974 from West Berlin to the censored East, even during the period when East Berliners could freely cross to the West and buy Western newspapers. Headed DIE FREIE BERLINER PRESSE MELDET ('The Free Berlin press announces'), it served to demonstrate to all that the communist East adopted censorship, and for a period in the early 1950s the East German Government erected a similar sign on the eastern side. In the foreground is part of the Potsdamer Platz S-Bahn station entrance.

The Havel lake at Glienicke Bridge, Berlin, 10 September 1959
It was not only on dry land that one encountered warning notices about the position of the border between East and West. Here, a notice states that the Zonengrenze (the border between West Berlin and East Germany proper) lies 75 metres away, and a West Berlin policeman keeps an eye on a group on a small boat to ensure that they do not stray into an unsafe area.

Glienicker Brücke (Glienicke Bridge), 10 September 1959
This is arguably the most famous bridge in Berlin, spanning Lake Havel between West Berlin and Potsdam. The notice warns that one is leaving the American Sector (West Berlin), but the other side of the bridge is not East Berlin, but East Germany proper. As a British Citizen I was allowed access to East Berlin but not to 'The Zone', as it was termed, without special permission. Several spy exchanges occurred here, notably that in 1962 of Gary Powers, the American U-2 pilot and Rudolf Abel, the Soviet spy. The bridge featured in the 1966 film *Funeral in Berlin* and the 2015 Spielberg film *Bridge of Spies*.

Glienicker Brücke (Glienicke Bridge), 10 September 1959
This looks from the centre of Glienicker Brücke, 'The Bridge of Spies', towards West Berlin. This is the first view that Gary Powers, the U-2 pilot who was shot down over the Soviet Union, would have had again of the West when in 1962 he was exchanged on this bridge for Rudolf Abel, the Soviet spy.

Zonal border near Glienicke Bridge, 10 September 1959

Before August 1961 one could cross between West and East Berlin without much formality, and notices advising of where the border lay were commonplace. However, to cross into East Germany proper (across the Zonal Border) one needed special permission, and this notice advises that East Germany lies ahead (but on this side of the street only) with the warning: 'Halt! Zonal Border. Use the other side of the street.' After 1961, the fence on the right would have been much more heavily fortified.

Zonal border near Glienicke Bridge, Berlin, 10 September 1959

These houses were in East Germany (not East Berlin), on the outer border of West Berlin. Until August 1961 the border was lightly fortified with barbed wire; the simplest way for these citizens to reach the location immediately outside their front windows without undergoing controls would be to travel to East Berlin several miles to the east, walk across to West Berlin and travel back again westwards.

Zonal border at Am Waldrand near Glienicke Bridge, Berlin, 10 September 1959
The zonal border between West Berlin and East Germany proper (not East Berlin) was lightly fenced off prior to August 1961, but any East German citizens wanting to flee to the West could simply travel to East Berlin, walk across to the west, and optionally then fly out to West Germany. On a journey to the edge of East Berlin, I could not see any indication of a marked boundary between East Berlin and East Germany. The far side of the barrier depicted is the borough of Potsdam.

Kurfürstendamm, West Berlin, 11 September 1959
On a sunny Friday afternoon in West Berlin the citizens promenading along the Kurfürstendamm could be excused for forgetting that they were living almost 100 miles behind the Iron Curtain, in an extraordinary oasis, enjoying things that were inaccessible to the citizens of the country that lay around them on all sides.

Potsdamer Platz, 11 September 1959
This shot gives a general view during the time when it was possible to walk across from the East to the West. From this vantage point on Leipziger Strasse in East Berlin can be seen how the electric news board in West Berlin (*see also page 20*) appeared to the citizens of the East. Although it was possible to walk across and buy Western newspapers, the billboard was a propaganda tool demonstrating the existence of censorship in the East. At this point, the white railings marked the border.

Leipziger Platz, East Berlin, 11 September 1959
These displays of the East German newspaper *Neues Deutschland* were commonplace in East Berlin, where no Western newspapers could be bought. The heading reads: 'Here speaks the Democratic Press.' The term 'democratic' was universally used in the East to describe the communist ideology. A common joke in the West was that the German Democratic Republic was neither a republic, nor democratic, nor German.

Gendarmenmarkt, East Berlin, 11 September 1959
This view of Deutscher Dom (the German Cathedral) in Gendarmenmarkt, with the rubble still remaining from war damage, also includes a distant view of Schinkel's concert hall the Schauspielhaus (*see page 46 for a description and photograph taken the following year*) and the top of Französischer Dom (the French Cathedral), also with its cupola missing. The two cathedrals in Gendarmenmarkt were almost identical.

Wartime rubble in Gendarmenmarkt, East Berlin, 11 September 1959
I came upon this remarkable scene in Gendarmenmarkt, now one of the main tourist squares of Berlin, which lies just south of Unter den Linden. The ruined church is one of two twin churches in this square. In contrast to the work done to repair war damage in West Berlin, the East German Government had not even begun to clear the rubble from the wartime devastation in this square. Gendarmenmarkt was originally constructed around 1688 as Lindenmarkt (the Lime Market). Its two almost identical churches are the French Church and the German Church. The square is also the location of a concert hall.

Friedrichstrasse/Unter den Linden, East Berlin, 11 September 1959

This is the junction of two of the most historically important streets of Berlin, in the area now known as Mitte. This shot looks across Unter den Linden and north along Friedrichstrasse. Unter den Linden originally dates from the seventeenth century; Friedrichstrasse, named after Frederick the Great, would become the location for Checkpoint Charlie two years after this photograph.

Friedrichstrasse/Unter den Linden junction, East Berlin, 11 September 1959

This is another view of the junction of these two main streets in the Mitte area. The camera looks along Friedrichstrasse, from south to north, and in the far distance is the bridge at Friedrichstrasse station, one of the main rail termini of Berlin. The motorcyclist is turning into Unter den Linden, the principal street of East Berlin, running from Brandenburger Tor, to the left of the camera, through to Marx-Engels-Platz and Berlin Cathedral to the far right.

Cafe Kranzler, Kurfürstendamm, West Berlin, 11 September 1959
Cafe Kranzler was arguably the most famous cafe on Kurfürstendamm, this location being known as Kranzler Eck (Kranzler Corner). The establishment was first opened by Johann Georg Kranzler in 1834 on Unter den Linden 25 at the corner with Friedrichstrasse (*see page 27*), and in 1932 the Kurfürstendamm location was opened. It still survives there, albeit in a greatly modified form.

Brandenburger Tor, Berlin, 11 September 1959
East Berlin began immediately behind the notice, not at the Brandenburger Tor itself as sometimes thought. It can be seen that a red flag is positioned on this side of the Tor. The view extends down Unter den Linden in East Berlin. In the distance is the Rotes Rathaus, the Red Town Hall (*see page 32*).

Strasse des 17 Juni and Brandenburger Tor, Berlin, 11 September 1959
Before August 1961 there were few restrictions on entering East Berlin, but the West Berlin police might ask for a friendly word, reminding travellers that there was no consular contact between East and West, and only limited telephone contact. After 1961 Westerners were strongly advised to leave details in the West if intending to travel to the East, and to confirm their return.

Soviet War Memorial and Reichstag, West Berlin, 11 September 1959
Ironically, the Soviet War Memorial lies in the Tiergarten, in what was West Berlin, in the British sector, and is guarded by Russian soldiers. It was erected in 1945 after a design by Mikhail Gorvitz, which takes the form of a curved edifice topped by the statue of a Russian soldier. In the distance is the Reichstag building, also in West Berlin. After the building of the Berlin Wall, the memorial had to be guarded against attack by West Berliners.

Pariser Platz 5a, East Berlin and Reichstag Building, West Berlin, 11 September 1959
This is a more close-up photograph of the building on page 15, the war-damaged headquarters of the Generalinspecteur für das Strassenwesen of the Deutsches Reich, address Pariser Platz 5a, which was demolished in 1960. The border with West Berlin lies between this building and the Reichstag building, which is undergoing renovation in the distance; the Reichstag lies entirely in West Berlin.

Unter den Linden, East Berlin, 11 September 1959
This almost looks like a scene from one of those science fiction movies where all human life has vanished. However, this was the scene I encountered after walking through the Brandenburg Gate in 1959, and this, Unter den Linden, is arguably East Berlin's main thoroughfare, contrasting markedly with the bustle of West Berlin's Kudamm. In the distance is Rotes Rathaus (the Red Town Hall).

Unter den Linden, East Berlin, 11 September 1959
This view is along Unter den Linden, looking east at the junction with Friedrichstrasse. The Museum für Deutsche Geschichte (Museum for German History) is not in the building opposite, which is marked 'Komische Oper' under the awning. The advertisement states that the Museum is '5 minutes from here' at Clara-Zetkin-Strasse 26 (now Dorotheenstrasse). In the distance can be seen the Rotes Rathaus (Red Town Hall) and the top of Berlin Cathedral.

Berliner Dom, East Berlin, 11 September 1959
Berliner Dom (Berlin Cathedral) on Museumsinsel (Museum Island) was inaugurated in 1905, and, although strictly speaking not a cathedral, is one of the main religious buildings of Berlin. It was damaged during the Second World War and reconstructed in the 1970s. This photograph, taken from Marx-Engels-Platz, also shows one of the distinctive East Berlin buses, 'Bus mit Schnauze' (bus with snout) as the Berliners termed it; these were almost identical to the West Berlin buses, in the same colour, except that the Western buses did not have the 'Schnauze'.

31

Rathausstrasse and Rotes Rathaus (Red Town Hall), East Berlin, 11 September 1959
The Rotes Rathaus was built in the 1860s, based on the design of the Town Hall of Torun, Poland. Its name has no political significance and refers to the colour of the brickwork. The building was damaged in the Second World War and rebuilt a few years before this photograph.

Rathausstrasse, East Berlin, 11 September 1959
This was the view from Rathausstrasse towards Alexanderplatz. A political slogan covers the length of the overhead bridge of the S-Bahn station. Also visible are two branches of HO (Handelsorganisation), the state retail outlet. The buildings on the left were demolished a few years later to make way for the construction of Fernsehturm (the Television Tower).

Alexanderplatz, East Berlin, 11 September 1959
This, the main public square of East Berlin (apart from Marx-Engels-Platz, used for parades), includes the headquarters of VEB Kombinat Minol, the state-owned petroleum outlet of East Germany, founded in 1956. The term VEB approximates to 'Limited' or 'Incorporated' and stands for Volkseigener Betrieb (Publicly-owned organisation). Also seen is an advertisement for *Am Abend*, the East German evening newspaper.

Deutsche Sporthalle, Stalinallee, East Berlin, 11 September 1959
The Deutsche Sporthalle (German Sport Hall) was hastily built in 1951 over a period of only five months, to a design by Richard Paulick. It was used to host several sporting events and exhibitions, but fell into disrepair during the 1960s owing to poor construction, as did parts of other buildings in this avenue. It was demolished in 1972. See page 43 for photographs of the statues outside the Sporthalle.

Stalinallee, East Berlin, 11 September 1959
Marching for socialism, these citizens of the German Democratic Republic no doubt supported the policies of Walter Ulbricht, their leader. Whether they would continue to support them in the years ahead is open to question.

Communist Rally, East Berlin, 11 September 1959
'... to institute the seven-year plan and the eradication of fascist and imperialist forces from Westberlin and the establishment of peace and harmony such as exists now in the democratic sector ...' (with a bullet in the back in a couple of years' time if you want to leave). I came upon this meeting somewhere near Stalinallee one afternoon.

Friedrichstrasse Station, 12 September 1959

Friedrichstrasse station was, and remains, one of the principal railway stations of Berlin, serving both the S-Bahn and U-Bahn. During the period of the Berlin Wall, it was the main rail connection to and from the West for non-Germans, who were subject to strict controls when entering or leaving the East. At the time of this shot, anyone could travel by rail or on foot between the two sectors of Berlin while undergoing few, if any, formalities. An advertisement for *Neues Deutschland*, the principal communist daily newspaper, is prominently sited on the railway bridge, and the ubiquitous political slogan boards are also in evidence.

Friedrichstrasse, East Berlin, 12 September 1959

This shot shows again, as remarked elsewhere, that almost everyone in East Berlin was carrying something. This looks north along Friedrichstrasse from a vantage point just north of Friedrichstrasse station. The U-Bahn station here, Oranienburger Tor, was a ghost station after August 1961, with trains running non-stop through it to West Berlin stations at each end of the line, and the station was removed from East Berlin maps. In the 1920s there were breweries on both sides of the street here.

Walter-Ulbricht-Stadion, Chausseestrasse 96, East Berlin, 12 September 1959
The Walter-Ulbricht-Stadion (Stadium) was opened in 1950 and hosted many sporting events including matches of SC Dynamo Berlin, where it acted as the home ground. The stadium was demolished in 1992 and after German reunification the address in Chausseestrasse became the location of a Government agency. Walter Ulbricht (1893–1973) was the First Secretary of the Socialist Unity Party and, in effect, the leader of East Germany at the time of this photograph.

At the border, Chausseestrasse, 12 September 1959
This is an example of how things were at the boundary between East and West Berlin before the Berlin Wall. There were virtually no controls on pedestrians, and the board advises that one will be leaving the 'democratic sector' 10 metres further on. The pile of bricks might be taken as an ominous symbol of things to come. After 1961 the whole of this area on the eastern side became a 'control zone' closed to the public.

Chausseestrasse, East Berlin, 12 September 1959
This looks southwards towards Friedrichstrasse and away from the border with West Berlin behind the camera. The border to which the cyclist is heading will, after 1961, become the Chausseestrasse checkpoint (*see page 68*). This thoroughfare will then have two major checkpoints, north and south, the southern one being Checkpoint Charlie.

Tauentzienstrasse, West Berlin, 12 September 1959
This is one of the earliest shots I took of Tauentzienstrasse (*see also page 53*), showing the entire street, and gives a good view of the tramline that used to run along this major shopping thoroughfare. On the extreme left is the corner of KaDeWe, the largest department store on mainland Europe. At the far end, the bombed Kaiser Wilhelm Memorial Church marks the junction of this street with Kurfürstendamm.

Witzleben S-Bahn station, West Berlin, 12 September 1959
Although the S-Bahn rail system ran throughout both sectors of Berlin, it was administered by the East German Government. The dilapidated state of the network can be seen here in the roof provided above the steps leading from the platform of Witzleben station in West Berlin. The roof above the steps subsequently collapsed and weeds covered the steps. The Persil advertisement on the platform referred to the East German product.

Budapester Strasse, West Berlin, 30 July 1960
It is said that in Berlin there is always building work going on, and this is still the case today. Unsurprisingly, only fifteen years after the war, much was being done to rebuild the city, and here new shops are rising from the rubble in Budapester Strasse, from the Kaiser Wilhelm Church in the distance up to the Hilton Hotel behind the camera.

The ruined Reichstag building, West Berlin, 31 July 1960
The Reichstag building, built between 1884 and 1894, served as the German Parliament building until 1933, when it was destroyed by fire. After the war, it was located in West Berlin, a few metres from the border with the East. After German reunification it was rebuilt according to the designs of the architect Norman Foster, and is noted for its dome, now a tourist attraction. It currently houses the German Parliament. In this shot the larger notice on the fence states that unauthorised entry is prohibited.

A HO store, East Berlin, 31 July 1960
Handelsorganisation, contracted to HO, was a retail business operated by the East German Government, which ran shops and hotels. Its stores were seen widely in East Berlin in competition with a similar enterprise, Konsum, insofar as competition can be said to have existed in a communist society. The stores sold a limited range of poorly made goods, and were depressing places to visit, reminiscent of wartime Co-operative stores in the UK. However, with the favourable rate at which East Marks could be bought in West Berlin, there were bargains to be found; I bought a decent watch there for 3 shillings (15p).

Stalinallee, East Berlin, 31 July 1960
Shopping in Stalinallee (later Karl-Marx-Allee). Most people encountered on the streets in East Berlin were carrying a bag of some sort. Stalinallee was a showcase boulevard built in the Soviet 'Wedding Cake' style, and the shops tended to display goods that were not generally available elsewhere in East Germany. The avenue was renamed in late 1961 after Stalin fell from favour.

Seven-Year Plan display, Stalinallee, East Berlin, 31 July 1960
This display in Stalinallee promotes the Seven-Year Plan of 1959–65. When the Five-Year Plan collapsed, the East German Government introduced this plan, which set the goal of increasing per capita production so that it surpassed that of West Germany by the end of 1961. The building of the Berlin Wall was not included in the measures. Similar plans were frequently instigated in other communist countries.

Filming in Stalinallee, East Berlin, 31 July 1960
Cinema films in East Germany were made under the auspices of the state film organisation DEFA (Deutsche Film-Aktiengesellschaft). It was decreed that films would not be made of the type made in Germany before the Second World War, seen as decadent, but would promote such topics as the joys of manual labour, the redistribution of land and the Seven Year Plan.

Behind the facade, East Berlin, 31 July 1960
The showpiece street of East Berlin was Stalinallee (now Karl-Marx-Allee). Built in the socialist 'Wedding Cake' style and almost 100 metres wide, it was intended to rival the boulevards of Western cities, and many of the shops sold wares that were not generally available elsewhere in East Germany. Although viewed from a distance it was impressive, the reality was somewhat different. As can be seen here, one had only to look behind the facades to see the desolation that was prevalent in much of East Berlin. During the 1960s the facings of the buildings began to peel off, and protective hoardings were erected to protect the public from falling debris.

Deutsche Sporthalle statues, Stalinallee,
East Berlin, 31 July 1960
These statues stood outside Deutsche
Sporthalle, the East German sport and
exhibition centre, which was built in 1951
and demolished in 1972 after falling into
disrepair (*see page 33*).

Potsdamer Platz, 31 July 1960

Before the building of the Berlin Wall, it was often confusing to determine in which sector a building lay. I took this photograph from a cafe on the Western side. I knew that the ruined building in the distance was Haus Vaterland, in East Berlin, and the roadway immediately outside the cafe was in the West, and so I thought it likely that the Post Office (Postamt) was in the West. On entering, intending to buy some West German stamps, I saw with dismay the sign 'Deutsche Demokratische Republik'. See page 70 for how this place looked after the Wall was built.

Thälmannplatz, East Berlin, 31 July 1960

Although I try to keep records of where and when I take photographs, with this one I did not record the location. However, when I posted it on the Flickr photographic website, it was identified by a Flickr member as Thälmannplatz (formerly Wilhelmplatz), named after Ernst Thälmann, the former leader of the German Communist Party. The square no longer exists, but the building with the Atlas sculpture is on the corner of Leipziger Strasse and Mauerstrasse. Another Flickr member was then able to identify where he had taken a shot, which had puzzled him for twenty-six years. He confirms that the building to the left of the lamppost is WMF-Haus at Leipziger Strasse 112.

Mohrenstrasse 65, East Berlin, 31 July 1960
This building was opened in September 1933 on the corner of Mauerstrasse as Thüringen-Haus, the headquarters of Thüringen, a state in central Germany. It is an example of how war-damaged buildings were left derelict by East Germany for as long as fifteen years after the war. It was later pulled down and the space used as a car park. A nondescript office block now occupies this space.

Between Mohrenstrasse and Kronenstrasse, East Berlin, 31 July 1960
I photographed this example of the devastation still remaining in East Berlin fifteen years after the war just west of Friedrichstrasse. The Art Nouveau building in the centre still exists and lies on the south side of Kronenstrasse. The building on the extreme left has been renovated as Mädler-Haus, at Friedrichstrasse 58. It is not now possible to photograph from this vantage point as modern apartment blocks cover this area.

Stadtmitte U-Bahn station, Mohrenstrasse, East Berlin, 31 July 1960
Behind the U-Bahn station stands the ruined Deutscher Dom on Gendarmenmarkt. After the Berlin Wall was built in 1961, the north–south U-Bahn trains bizarrely still ran through Stadtmitte and other East Berlin stations. They stopped only at West Berlin stations at each end of the line, but also at Friedrichstrasse in East Berlin, where passengers could leave and pass through rigorous controls before being allowed into East Berlin. At other stations, trains ran through non-stop, with People's Police on the platforms ensuring that nobody escaped through the tunnels.

Schauspielhaus, Gendarmenmarkt, East Berlin, 31 July 1960
Originally named Schauspielhaus when opened in 1821, to a design by Karl Schinkel, this concert hall on Gendarmenmarkt was badly damaged during the Second World War along with several other buildings in this square, and this damage was still evident when I took this shot in 1960. The building was later rebuilt by the East German Government and was reopened in 1984 as the Konzerthaus Berlin, the answer to West Berlin's Philharmonie.

Gendarmenmarkt, East Berlin, 31 July 1960
Although the East German Government had not begun to repair this church fifteen years after the war, or even clear the rubble from the square nearby, they had found time to rename the street in memory of politician Otto Nuschke (1883–1957), who had received the Patriotic Order of the DDR.

Near Gendarmenmarkt, East Berlin, 31 July 1960
The ruin of one of the twin churches on Gendarmenmarkt, together with a banner espousing socialism. One of the by-products of socialism as practised in the DDR seems to have been that the two churches were left untouched in ruins for over fifteen years, and the rubble on the ground had not even been cleared (*see page 26*).

Kaiser Wilhelm Memorial Church, West
Berlin, 31 July 1960
This church was built in the 1890s,
and was dedicated to Kaiser Wilhelm
I (1797–1888). It was finally opened in
1906. In November 1943 it was badly
damaged in an air raid, and much
controversy ensued after the war as to
what course of action to take. It was
finally decided to retain the ruined tower,
for which Berliners had much affection
(referring to it as 'the hollow tooth'), as
a symbol of the futility of war. In 1963
a new belfry and chapel were opened
alongside. The church was undoubtedly
the focal point of West Berlin.

The Victory Column, West Berlin,
31 July 1960
The Victory Column was built in the
1860s to commemorate the victory of
Prussia in the Danish-Prussian War. It
originally stood in front of the Reichstag
Building but in 1939 was relocated to
its current site at Grosser Stern (Great
Star), a junction of several avenues,
including Strasse des 17 Juni, leading
to Brandenburger Tor and towards East
Berlin. This avenue commemorates the
uprising in East Berlin against the East
German regime on 17 June 1953, and
somewhat provocatively bears this name
right up to the East Berlin border.

Schloss Bellevue, West Berlin, 1 August 1960
Schloss Bellevue in the Tiergarten was built in 1786 to a design by Philipp Boumann as the summer residence of Prince Augustus Ferdinand of Prussia. It was damaged during the Second World War and restored a few years before this photograph was taken, to be used as a residence of the West German President when he was in Berlin. At this time the capital of West Germany was Bonn.

Soviet War Memorial, Strasse des 17 Juni, West Berlin, 1 August 1960
This is the main inscription on the Soviet War Memorial, which somewhat ironically lay in West Berlin. It reads: 'Eternal glory to the heroes fallen in battles with German fascist invaders for the freedom and independence of the Soviet Union.'

Zeughaus, Unter den Linden, East Berlin,
1 August 1960
The Zeughaus, built around 1700, is the oldest
building on Unter den Linden and stands at
the extreme eastern end of that boulevard near
the Berliner Dom (Cathedral) and what was
Marx-Engels-Platz. It served initially as an arsenal,
and later as a military museum. It was damaged in
the Second World War, and was later used by the
East German Government as the Museum of German
History (as seen through communist eyes). After
German reunification, it still serves in a similar
capacity.

Tram with political slogan, East Berlin, 1 August 1960
Political slogans festooned not only the sides of buildings in East Berlin, but also public
transport. Here, the message is one of many calling for West Berlin to be a 'free city'. Whether
the citizens would wish to experience the sort of freedom enjoyed by East Berliners is arguable.
At the time of this photograph, trams operated in both sectors of Berlin, but now they are seen
only in the eastern part of Berlin.

Communist propaganda, East Berlin, 1 August 1960

Political slogans across buildings and on public transport were commonplace in East Berlin, usually in yellow on red backgrounds. One slogan in both of these photographs states: 'We demand a peace treaty with both German states and a demilitarised free city of West Berlin.' The latter is, as usual in the DDR, rendered as 'Westberlin'. Whether the DDR also demand a demilitarised free East Germany is not stated.

Reichstag building and tram,
1 August 1960
This depicts a situation that would
have been impossible after the building
of the Berlin Wall. The Reichstag
building, of which the rear is shown
here, lay entirely in West Berlin. The
tram lines were part of the East Berlin
tram network, and so it would have
been possible for anyone to alight
from the tram here and walk a few
steps into West Berlin. After 1961 the
Berlin Wall was built almost exactly
along the line of this tramline. One of
the photographs depicts an East Berlin
notice stating that the 'democratic
sector' ends 36 metres further on, i.e.
beyond the tramline but before the
Reichstag. I am informed that the
number 70 tram was extended as far
as this point in 1958, and ran until the
Berlin Wall was built in August 1961.

In Kurfürstendamm, West Berlin, 2 August 1960
Tourism existed, rather than flourished, in West Berlin for those who sought an interesting holiday different from lying on a beach. Coach tours included Berlin by Night, West Berlin alone, and combined West and East Berlin. The guide on the East Berlin section was an obedient party member, and inevitably the tour included visits to USSR-connected locations. After August, 1961, one's movements were closely monitored. Tours were also available to Potsdam in East Germany, where the monitoring was even more stringent.

Tauentzienstrasse, West Berlin, 2 August 1960
Tauentzienstrasse is a major shopping thoroughfare, which forms the continuation of Kurfürstendamm on the opposite side of the Kaiser Wilhelm Memorial Church (seen here in the distance). It contains several large department stores, including KaDeWe, off-camera to the left, the largest department store on mainland Europe. The tramlines seen here down the centre of the road no longer exist, as trams operate only in the east of the city.

53

Airlift memorial, Tempelhof Airport, West Berlin, 2 August 1960
Luftbrückendenkmal (the Airlift Memorial), designed by Eduard Ludwig, stands outside Tempelhof Airport and commemorates the Berlin Airlift of 1948–49, when the Soviets cut land access to West Berlin and the city had to be supplied using the three air corridors. The three arcs at the top facing west represent the three air corridors connecting West Berlin to the cities of Hanover, Hamburg and Frankfurt in West Germany.

Rathaus Schöneberg (City Hall), West Berlin, 2 August 1960
Built around 1914, this City Hall is perhaps best known as the location of US President John Kennedy's 'Ich bin ein Berliner' speech of June 1963. It served as West Berlin's City Hall during the Cold War, because the Rotes Rathaus was in East Berlin; after reunification it again became the City Hall for the borough of Schöneberg. A few days after Kennedy's assassination in November 1963, the square outside the Hall was renamed John-F.-Kennedy-Platz.

Friedrichstrasse, 3 August 1960

The American authorities question the driver of a BMW bubble car with a West Berlin licence plate (B-) that has just come from East Berlin. Across the street, and a few steps inside East Berlin, is the headquarters of *Neue Zeit*, the Marxist review magazine founded in 1883.

Friedrichstrasse sector border (Later Checkpoint Charlie), 3 August 1960

This looks north along Friedrichstrasse from West Berlin into the East. The cyclist is about to cross Zimmerstrasse, along which ran the white line marking the border after Checkpoint Charlie came into being. When I took this shot it was not appreciated that this location would become world famous, and although many photographs of Checkpoint Charlie now exist, there are probably few which show how this crossing appeared before August 1961.

Ruins of Anhalter Bahnhof, West Berlin, 3 August 1960
This was one of the more bizarre experiences of my visits to Berlin. I entered the ruin of this railway terminus and discovered a tunnel, which I explored. As it was very near the border with the East I imagined with some trepidation that the other end might surface in East Berlin. However, after crawling along it for some time I found that the other end emerged near the border but still in the West. It was later pointed out to me that the tunnel was constructed in 1927 from the station to connect to the basement of the nearby Excelsior Hotel.

Near Haus Vaterland, Potsdamer Platz, Berlin, 3 August 1960

Although at first sight these photographs may seem of little interest, I was told by an expert on the history of Potsdamer Platz that these were the closest shots of the damaged Haus Vaterland from this era that he had seen. Taken a few yards into East Berlin, it was not possible to approach this area after the building of the Berlin Wall. This is also the site of the old Potsdamer Bahnhof (railway station). Behind the worker in the white shirt is the memorial to Karl Liebknecht, co-founder of the German Communist Party. This memorial still stands in present-day Berlin.

Potsdamer Platz, Berlin, 3 August 1960

East German boards announcing the end of the 'democratic sector' after so many metres were commonplace before the building of the Berlin Wall. In these two overlapping shots, taken almost simultaneously, the white railings along the pavement edge marked the border, and the black board stated 'British Sector'. The Coca-Cola and other Western advertisement signs confirm that the shops are in West Berlin. On the view along Potsdamer Strasse, the change in road surface probably marks the actual border, which has turned through a right angle just past the black board.

Stresemannstrasse, 3 August 1960

In Stresemannstrasse, the determination of the location of the zig-zag line between East and West Berlin was problematic, to say the least. It also produced a rare phenomenon – Western advertisements about a metre into East German territory. The buildings on the right are in West Berlin, but the pavement (and hence the space above it) is in the East. At the corner with Niederkirchner Strasse, ahead on the left, the large notification board is in the West, whereas the small side-on one in front of it is a DDR board advising the end of the 'democratic sector'. The sentry post further ahead on the right is in West Berlin.

Potsdamer Platz, Berlin, 3 August 1960

Many thousands of photographs were taken of this view after the building of the Berlin Wall from the viewing platform in Potsdamer Platz (*see page 76*), but possibly few exist from the years before, since there was little reason to photograph this somewhat mundane, nondescript scene. This looks along Leipziger Strasse into East Berlin from just inside West Berlin at Potsdamer Platz. The newspaper displayed on the board near the news-stand is almost certainly *Neues Deutschland*, the East German daily newspaper.

Near Potsdamer Platz, East Berlin, 3 August 1960
This faces west in the days when traffic moved freely between West and East Berlin. The Volkswagen vehicles bear West Berlin licence plates. In the background is the ruined Haus Vaterland (Fatherland House), which lay on Eastern territory, with Stresemannstrasse off to the left. Potsdamer Platz and the border with West Berlin is off-camera to the right. Haus Vaterland, built in 1928, was a major entertainment centre housing among other attractions Cafe Piccadilly, the largest cafe in the world. It was demolished in 1976.

Tempelhof Airport, West Berlin, 3 August 1960
Tempelhof was the principal airport that connected West Berlin to West Germany during the Cold War period. Aircraft had to stay within strictly defined and agreed air corridors that linked West Berlin to Hamburg, Hanover and Frankfurt. In later years a direct London–West Berlin service operated using one of the corridors. Zentralflughafen Tempelhof-Berlin was opened in 1927 and was unusual in that it was located in the centre of a city. It closed in 2008, and became a refugee centre in 2015.

After the Wall

Anti-communist propaganda, Tiergarten, West Berlin, 25 August 1962
Although most political slogans in Berlin were anti-West and in East Berlin, here is
an example of a protest in the Tiergarten in West Berlin against Walter Ulbricht, the
East German leader. The somewhat odd barbed wire fence across the footpath, with
the *'Betreten verboten'* notice, suggests that the footpath on the far side of the fence is
technically on East Berlin territory, even though the roadway may not be. The Berlin Wall,
built entirely on East Berlin territory some distance from the actual border, would in that
event have been only a short distance away.

Near the Soviet War Memorial, West Berlin, 25 August 1962
Although the public were normally allowed to access this road – the Strasse des 17 Juni,
up to Brandenburger Tor – there was heightened political tension during this period,
including incidents such as the Russians intimidating the West Berliners with supersonic
booms from aircraft. At this time the West Berlin authorities controlled access to this road
because of the location of the Russian War Memorial, seen here, which was ironically
located in West Berlin. Note the barbed wire entanglements protecting the memorial.

Berlin Philharmonic Orchestra, West Berlin, 25 August 1962

The Berlin Philharmonic Orchestra, formerly under the renowned conductor Herbert von Karajan, is frequently referred to as the finest orchestra in the world. Its permanent home is now the Philharmonie concert hall, which was opened in West Berlin in 1963 very close to the Berlin Wall. Prior to the building of Philharmonie the orchestra held concerts in a number of venues, and I took this photograph in the Free University Building near Zoo Station, after rain had prevented the concert being held that afternoon in the Jagdschloss Grunewald.

Wannsee S-Bahn Station, West Berlin, 25 August 1962

Wannsee S-Bahn station was on the edge of West Berlin near the 'Zonengrenze' (the border between West Berlin and East Germany proper). This notice advises passengers travelling in the direction of Potsdam in East Germany to warn fellow passengers that they may be detained if they are not authorised to travel outside West Berlin.

Wannsee, West Berlin, 25 August 1962
One of the major leisure activities of West Berliners and those tourists prepared to visit the city was to spend a day on one of the many lakes that cover the outlying reaches of Berlin. The city has some of the most extensive urban spans of lakes and forests to be found anywhere, and the lakes reached as far as Glienicke Bridge, the border with East Germany, and even beyond, although any further access by West Berlin boats was not possible. A big plus was that the inexpensive travelcard covering travel by bus and U-Bahn also included the boats.

Kurfürstendamm, West Berlin, 27 August 1962
Kurfürstendamm was the principal shopping street of West Berlin, and after reunification now rivals Unter den Linden for that title. I took this shot at around 6 in the morning and it evokes something of the flavour of the laid-back, peaceful nature of this boulevard. It is a delightful place to saunter, without the crowds and bustle of, say, the Champs Elysees. Another advantage is that there is not the current obsession with redesigning things that work perfectly well. One can return ten years later and still find the same shops and restaurants. Even the street signs have the same design after fifty years.

Kurfürstendamm, West Berlin, 27 August 1962
This shot includes the Hotel am Zoo, Haus Wien (the building with the pointed roof) and the Hotel Kempinski. The Hotel am Zoo (now the Hotel Zoo) was built in 1891 as a private residence, and was converted to a hotel in 1911. Haus Wien was a renowned Austrian restaurant. Hotel Kempinski was the flagship of Europe's oldest hotel group and remains as one of Berlin's leading hotels.

Kurfürstendamm U-Bahn, West Berlin, 27 August 1962, 6.24 a.m.
The Berlin U-Bahn metro system is one of the most efficient one could hope to use. The ticketing system, being fixed-fare, requires no exit controls; the illuminated destination boards, using the Paris system of indicating the line's terminus station (here Leopoldplatz), are logical. As to the positioning of indicators, a bright child of eight could tell you to position them all at the same height, and well spaced apart. In London, they are placed at any height the fitter chooses, and many obscure one another when viewed from along the platform.

Memorial to Ida Siekmann, Bernauer Strasse, 27 August 1962
Ida Siekmann leapt from her third-floor flat in Bernauer Strasse to reach West Berlin about a week after the sector border was sealed. She died a few days later of her injuries, on 22 August 1961. On this side of Bernauer Strasse the buildings were in the Eastern sector and the pavement in West Berlin. Since those early days, as can be seen, the inhabitants of the buildings had been moved out and the windows bricked up.

Berlin Wall inside window at Bernauer Strasse, 27 August 1962
The windows of the apartments in Bernauer Strasse were famously bricked up shortly after the Berlin Wall was built, and this is a close-up of one of the windows. The procedure was deemed necessary by the East German regime because tenants were jumping out of the windows to reach the pavement, which was in West Berlin. Several of the refugees were killed by trying to escape in this way.

Berlin Wall at Bernauer Strasse, 27 August 1962
Here the Berlin Wall divides a cross street, Brunnenstrasse, at Bernauer Strasse, the street at which windows were bricked up to prevent escapers from the East. The frequently seen graffiti 'KZ' (Konzentrationslager = Concentration Camp) can be seen here. The U-Bahn station is Bernauer Strasse, Line U8, a ghost station with trains running through it non-stop, each end of the U8 line being in West Berlin. East German police were stationed on the platforms to prevent refugees from escaping through the tunnels.

Bernauer Strasse, Berlin, 27 August 1962

This is arguably the most well-known of the locations of the Berlin Wall, and where a number of deaths occurred as a result of people fleeing from the East. The buildings are in East Berlin, whereas the pavement is in the West. Shortly after the Wall was built, refugees used to jump from the windows on to the street below. The authorities then removed the inhabitants of the buildings and bricked up the windows. Note that one brick space was left open so that the People's Police could observe the activity in the street below.

In Bernauer Strasse, West Berlin, 27 August 1962

This notice, headed MURDER, asks 'Who knows the shooter?' and offers a 3,000 Deutsche Mark reward (then about £300) for the capture of the border guard who shot a refugee swimming across the River Spree (i.e. on West Berlin territory) while attempting to escape from East Berlin.

Crossing point at Chausseestrasse/Liesenstrasse, 27 August 1962

This is the same location as the photograph on page 68. A French border guard on the right (in the French sector) watches the two East German guards in conversation. The white line denoting the border is just visible; the border crosses between the French and East German guards, and then turns right through 90 degrees and along the pavement, enabling the Wall to be built a few metres behind it. Thus, East Berlin is both in front of and to the right of the French official.

Berlin Wall near Chausseestrasse, 27 August 1962

'Steckbrief' denotes a 'Wanted' poster. This individual is wanted for murder, and its positioning on the Berlin Wall would indicate that this is probably for a wanted East German border guard who shot a potential escapee after the refugee had reached Western territory, thus committing a crime in West Berlin. Note the white line marking the actual border, and that the area beyond it (in East Berlin) is unweeded.

At Chausseestrasse Checkpoint, Berlin, 27 August 1962
The East German border guards question the inhabitants of a West Berlin-registered car (licence plate begins B-). Non-Germans such as UK and US citizens were not allowed to use Chausseestrasse; they had to enter and exit East Berlin via either Checkpoint Charlie or by train at Friedrichstrasse station.

Camaraderie at the Wall, Chausseestrasse, East Berlin, 27 August 1962
I was able to take this shot without being approached by the People's Police because I was standing about a metre inside West Berlin. The border guards are clearly enjoying their work. The officer standing on this site of the Wall was obviously a very trusted individual, and it is unclear whether the others would have been given orders to shoot him if he had made a run for it.

Above: Berlin Wall at Boyenstrasse, 27 August 1962
In Boyenstrasse, the entire pavement lay in East Berlin,
even though it was on the Western side of the Wall. The
small barrier across the pavement is to indicate that it is
unwise to cross it, since if anything untoward were to occur
there, the Western police (from the French sector) would
in theory not be authorised to access the territory. Later
photographs show that the buildings on both sides of the
street were demolished.

Right: Schloss Charlottenburg, West Berlin, 27 August 1962
Schloss Charlottenburg (Charlottenburg Palace) was
initially built between 1695 and 1713 under the commission
of Sophia Charlotte, the consort of King Friedrich I of
Prussia, and underwent much expansion in future years. It
was badly damaged in 1943 during the Second World War
and was later restored, although at one time the damage
was thought to be so serious that it would have to be
demolished. The palace and baroque gardens are open to
the public.

Below right: Funkturm, West Berlin, 27 August 1962
The 150-metre-high Funkturm (Radio Tower) was opened
in 1926, and is now the focus of a leisure area. The road
sign commemorates the second Secretary-General of the
United Nations, who was killed in a plane crash in Africa
while still in office in September 1961. I am informed
that this road sign probably had a short life because it is
grammatically incorrect. The rules in Germany governing
place names (whether they are spelt as one word or split
and whether they have hyphens) are strictly adhered to,
and errors are not tolerated (*see page 86*).

Kurfürstendamm, West Berlin, 27 August 1962
The Kudamm is one of those Continental boulevards where citizens go out in the evenings to stroll and maybe sit and have a drink, watching the passing scene, in a way which would not happen in, say, Oxford Street in London; however, one must take into account that many Berliners live within a stone's throw of the centre, whereas in London they do not. This is the eastern end of the Kudamm, near the Kaiser Wilhelm Memorial Church.

Potsdamer Platz, Berlin, 28 August 1962
This is the same scene that I photographed in 1960 (*see page 44*) when I was confused about whether the Post Office (Postamt) lay in West or in East Berlin. It now lies in the Eastern control zone, forbidden for anyone to enter except Eastern border guards.

Potsdamer Platz, Berlin, 28 August 1962
This shot looks across to Stresemannstrasse (*see pages 59 and 74*), receding from the camera. As mentioned elsewhere, the border was somewhat bizarre here, cutting across the street so that some sections of the street are in West and some in East Berlin. In the distance were the ruins of Anhalter Bahnhof (*see page 56*). The ruin of Haus Vaterland is on the right.

Potsdamer Platz, Berlin, 28 August 1962
This shot includes a curious anomaly, which I found nowhere else on the border. The notice is a DDR sign facing East and denotes the number of metres to the actual border, or to the 'end of the democratic sector', but it is marooned on the Western side of the Wall; it must itself obviously lie in East Berlin. A souvenir hunter could presumably have removed it without any action from West Berlin police. In the distance is the Reichstag (with flag), which lay entirely within West Berlin.

Judith at the Berlin Wall, 28 August 1962
Judith looks longingly into the socialist paradise.
Realising that her application to live in the democratic
republic would almost certainly be turned down,
she took the next best option. She married me the
following year.

Left and below: US Army control point at Checkpoint
Charlie, Berlin, 28 August 1962
This checkpoint (US Army because it was the American
Sector) served to monitor the crossings of citizens entering
and leaving East Berlin. Although it was not compulsory,
one was strongly advised to register if entering the East,
and to advise them on one's return. This was because
most Western countries did not recognise East Germany
as a sovereign state, with no respective embassies, and
communications between West and East Berlin were
tentative. Shown also in the photograph below is the
Neue Zeit East German newspaper building.

Checkpoint Charlie, Friedrichstrasse, Berlin, 29 August 1962
Two shots of Checkpoint Charlie at 7.20 a.m., when few civilians were about. Checkpoint Charlie, the most famous of the East–West crossing points, came into being at the junction of Friedrichstrasse and Zimmerstrasse after the building of the Berlin Wall in August 1961. Its name derives from the letter C in the phonetic alphabet, following the lesser-known Alpha and Bravo checkpoints. It was the only foot and vehicle crossing point for foreigners, and the location of a major East–West standoff in 1961. It is now a major tourist attraction.

Wilhelmstrasse, 29 August 1962

This bleak landscape shows the view northwards from the West Berlin end of Wilhelmstrasse at its junction with Kochstrasse. The building on the left served as the headquarters of the Luftwaffe during the Second World War, and other administrative buildings of the Reich were in this street, so that the term Wilhelmstrasse came into use to denote the German Nazi Government. The continuation northwards beyond the Berlin Wall was renamed Otto-Grotewohl-Strasse in 1964 in honour of the first East German Prime Minister, who died in that year (*see page 90*). Wilhelmstrasse continues northwards until it reaches Unter den Linden, near Brandenburger Tor, where now the British Embassy is located.

Stresemannstrasse, Berlin, 29 August 1962

This aspect of Stresemannstrasse is opposite to that on page 59, which I took in 1960 before the Berlin Wall, and which explains that the position of the border is complex on this street. The small buildings in the foreground (which were shops) are in West Berlin, but the adjoining pavement is in East Berlin, despite the fact that it is on the Western side of the wall. This explains why the board warns that you are leaving the American Sector at this point, and why the pavement is roped off and is in an unkempt and unweeded state. In the distance are the ruins of Haus Vaterland.

Corner of Stresemannstrasse and Niederkirchner Strasse, Berlin, 29 August 1962
This looks across Stresemannstrasse to the corner with Niederkirchner Strasse. The white sector boundary advice board and advertisement pillar can be seen in my photograph on page 59, taken in 1960 before the erection of the Berlin Wall and seen from a point further to the left down Stresemannstrasse. The building shown is Abgeordnetenhaus, a former government building. Niederkirchner Strasse is also notorious for having been the headquarters of the Gestapo and SS in Nazi Germany.

Potsdamer Platz, 29 August 1962
The Coca-Cola sign stands almost as an act of defiance against the East. The symbol was seen in the DDR as the arch-symbol of Western decadence, and was never encountered in those years behind the Iron Curtain. The disused S-Bahn station entrance would almost certainly have been situated on East Berlin territory.

Potsdamer Platz and Stresemannstrasse, East Berlin, 29 August 1962
This shot looks from Potsdamer Platz towards Stresemannstrasse and is approximately at
right angles to the one I took a few seconds later towards Leipziger Strasse. On the right
is the ruin of Haus Vaterland, the pre-war entertainment centre. A short distance along
Stresemannstrasse the Berlin Wall doubles back, so that the remainder of the street is in
West Berlin.

East Berlin from Potsdamer Platz, 29 August 1962
This is the view from Potsdamer Platz looking along Leipziger Strasse, which is where the
East Berlin tram can just be made out. Off-camera to the left is the site of Hitler's bunker.
Although Westerners could approach the Berlin Wall up to any distance, East Berliners
were kept beyond a control zone, which extended approximately up to the position of the
tram. The X-shaped constructions are tank traps. When this shot was taken, the Berlin
Wall was still made of crude blocks topped with barbed wire; later it was replaced with a
more solidly built barrier.

Potsdamer Platz, Berlin, 29 August 1962

The Wall at Potsdamer Platz. The white line may have been a stop line for trams rather than having any political significance, although the border was always a few steps to the west of the Wall itself so that it lay entirely in East Berlin. Trams on the western side ran up to a few metres of the actual boundary, as shown below.

'Endstation', Potsdamer Platz, 29 August 1962

There is certainly a good reason not to extend this route. This is a West Berlin tram that has reached its terminus. The driver is leaning out and using a mechanical points-changer pole. The destination board reads Finckensteinallee, which is a region of south-west Berlin that was the earliest trial ground of Werner von Siemens' introduction of the first electric trams in the world in 1881.

Philharmonie under construction, West Berlin, 29 August 1962

See page 83 for photographs of this concert hall in 1964 after it was inaugurated, and page 62 for a photograph I took of the orchestra in 1962 at the Free University Building. I attended a concert here in 1964 and was struck by the efficient way in which things were organised. After the concert, patrons found twelve empty double-decker buses waiting outside to transport them to the city centre. In London, crowds exiting the Albert Hall, with almost twice the capacity, would find a single bus stop.

The 'Egg' on Kurfürstendamm, West Berlin, 29 August 1962

All Berliners are familiar with the 'egg', which stands on the north side of Kurfürstendamm, some considerable distance from the Kaiser Wilhelm Memorial Church (in the distance). It has been here on all of my visits to Berlin, and I hope it will be there for many more. A characteristic of Berlin is that things often tend to stay the same, without the fashion for updating, modernising and redesigning that seems to be considered so necessary nowadays.

Kurfürstendamm, West Berlin, 29 August 1962
This looks eastwards some distance from the Kaiser Wilhelm Memorial Church (seen in the distance) and depicts some of the many showcases that have always been an attractive feature of this boulevard. Exhibiting usually a range of upmarket goods such as jewellery, carpets and cosmetics, they guide customers towards nearby establishments, often in side streets off the main avenue.

Kurfürstendamm, West Berlin, 29 August 1962
This is the eastern end of Kurfürstendamm and depicts the bombed Kaiser Wilhelm Memorial Church and new extension. Also shown is the Gloria Palast cinema, one of the principal Berlin cinemas. Berlin has always been noted for its connection with cinema, and hosts an annual International Film Festival (Berlinale). The Gloria Palast opened in 1926, and in 1930 the premiere of Dietrich's *Blue Angel* was held here. Lilli Palmer, on the current poster, is perhaps not related to Harry Palmer. The cinema was bombed in 1943, rebuilt in 1953, and finally closed in 1998.

Kurfürstendamm, West Berlin, 29 August 1962
A typical street scene in West Berlin. This is the eastern end of Kurfürstendamm, the principal shopping street of the Western Sector, and Berlin's answer to the Champs Elysees. On the left is the ruined Kaiser Wilhelm Memorial Church, bombed in 1943 and left as a memorial to the futility of war, and next to it is the modern church, consecrated in 1961. The U-Bahn station seen here also opened in that year. The chequered building in the distance was the Berlin Hilton Hotel.

DDR State Council Building, Marx-Engels-Platz, East Berlin, 23 June 1964
This building was constructed between 1962 and 1964 at the address Marx-Engels-Platz 1 (now Schlossplatz), in what is now the Mitte district; it served as the seat of the State Council of East Germany, and was used for official and diplomatic functions. The scaffolding on the left-hand side indicates that when I took this shot it may have been in the final stages of construction.

Apartment blocks being built in Alexanderstrasse, East Berlin, 23 June 1964
This is Alexanderstrasse, near Karl-Marx-Allee (formerly Stalinallee), looking south. Most buildings in East Berlin were built in the Stalinist 'Brutalist' style, characterised by Karl-Marx-Allee itself and seen in many other communist countries. The tram followed a route from Kreuzberg; this tramline was abandoned later in the 1960s.

Karl-Marx-Allee, East Berlin, 23 June 1964
This photograph, taken from the Alexanderplatz end of Karl-Marx-Allee (formerly Stalinallee), shows one of the few architecturally admired buildings erected by the East German regime – the cinema Kino International, on the extreme left, which opened in 1963. Trams operated in a loop line in this location during the 1960s; they have recently been restored.

Hotel Berolina, Karl-Marx-Allee, East Berlin, 23 June 1964
The Hotel Berolina, designed by Josef Kaiser, was opened in 1963 and was one of the leading hotels in East Berlin. It had 375 rooms and several restaurants. The hotel closed in 1996. On the right is the cinema Kino International, which also opened in 1963, and is still in use today as a cinema and conference centre.

Border fortifications on Humboldthafen waterway, 23 June 1964
I took this shot from an S-Bahn train about to enter Lehrter Bahnhof (now Berlin Hauptbahnhof), and it may not have been possible to photograph this location otherwise, as it was within a DDR control zone. The entire waterway lay in East Berlin, but the East German regime could not have built the fortifications on the far side, as that bank was West Berlin territory. The large building is the background was the Swiss Embassy.

Philharmonie, West Berlin, 24 June 1964
Philharmonie, the concert hall that is
now the home of the Berlin Philharmonic
Orchestra, was opened in the Tiergarten
in October 1963, the year before I took
this photograph, within a few steps of
the Berlin Wall. The old Philharmonie
was destroyed during the Second World
War in 1944, and until this building was
opened the Philharmonic Orchestra gave
concerts in a number of venues. See
page 62 for a photograph I took of the
orchestra in 1962 at the Free University
Building, and page 78 for a photograph of
Philharmonie under construction in the
same year.

Ernst-Reuter-Platz, West Berlin, 23 June 1964
A glimpse of the author desperately trying to appear relaxed while taking a break from photographing the city in Ernst-Reuter-Platz. A colleague has remarked that he looks as if he is waiting for his controller to approach and tender the correct password.

Robert Kennedy and Willy Brandt, Kurfürstendamm, West Berlin, 25 June 1964
I came upon this motorcade purely by chance while walking along the Kurfürstendamm, and needed to be very quick with my camera. Robert Kennedy was in Berlin to mark the first anniversary of US President John F. Kennedy's famous 'I am a Berliner' speech on 26 June 1963, and gave a speech from the same platform. Robert Kennedy was assassinated in Los Angeles in June 1968. Willy Brandt, the mayor of West Berlin at the time, later became Chancellor of West Germany.

Checkpoint Charlie, Friedrichstrasse, Berlin, 24 December 1964

The view from West Berlin across Checkpoint Charlie on Christmas Eve 1964. The propaganda board (somewhat unusually, in English) claims an 'Acheson-Adenauer-Dulles conspiracy'. Dean Acheson (1896–1971), an American statesman, was more or less a private citizen at this time; Konrad Adenauer (1876–1967) was an ex-Chancellor of West Germany; John Foster Dulles (1888–1959), a US ex-Secretary of State, had been dead for over five years.

Above: Relaxing by the lake, West Berlin,
25 June 1964
Life in Berlin was not all centred on politics. More
than most cities of its size, Berlin possesses a huge
area devoted to greenery and lakes. It was possible to
spend all day on the many boat trips traversing the
lakes without duplicating any journey, and amazingly
the daily rail and bus travelcard issued at the time
included these trips. At many locations on the
lakeside were cafes serving sumptuous delicacies, for
which Berliners are famous. This shot gives a flavour
of how the citizens took advantage of life in their city.

Left: At Checkpoint Charlie, Berlin,
24 December 1964
'No, sonny, I am sure that Father Christmas didn't
come past where I am.'

Berlin Wall at Luckauer Strasse, 24 December 1964
Luckauer Strasse is a street off Oranienstrasse in
Kreuzberg, a district south of Mitte. It is named
after Luckau, a German town, and so according
to the vagaries of German street nomenclature, it
must be rendered as two separate words (unlike
Oranienstrasse). The derelict building behind the
propaganda board demonstrates how the East
Germans left war-damaged edifices untouched nearly
twenty years after the war.

Berlin Wall at Oberbaumbrücke, East Berlin, 24 December 1964
I came across this curious place at Oberbaumbrücke, the bridge over the River Spree, which formed the border between West and East Berlin in this part of the city. The Wall was not heavily fortified, and elderly people could occasionally be seen on the Eastern side. I later learned that this was the crossing point for disabled citizens and those over sixty-five, who were allowed to cross to the West as they were no longer useful to the East German economy. There would have been much heavier fortifications at the far end of the bridge to restrict other East Berliners from accessing this area.

Berlin Wall near Wildenbruchstrasse, 24 December 1964
High watchtowers such as these were not the norm along
the Berlin Wall. The Wall was always built some metres
inside East Berlin, and so these cars are presumably
technically on East Berlin territory, and therefore immune
from the attention of West Berlin parking attendants!

Bouchestrasse, East Berlin, 24 December 1964
The notice warns that the pavement between Harzer
Strasse and Heidelberger Strasse technically belongs to
Treptow, part of the 'Soviet occupied sector' of Berlin.
The Berlin Wall was always built some metres within
East Berlin territory. Although the notice probably lies
on East Berlin territory, it is obviously Western in origin
because of the use of the term 'Soviet occupied sector'.
The East German regime maintained that their sector
was part of a German republic, not territory occupied by
the USSR.

Corner of
Wildenbruchstrasse and
Heidelberger Strasse,
Berlin, 24 December 1964
The apartments on the left
were in West Berlin. The
dilapidated walkway on
the right, being untended
and close to the Wall, was
probably in East Berlin. The
sector information board,
referring to the 'Westsektor',
is highly unusual and may
date from shortly after the
city was divided.

Kurfürstendamm, West Berlin, 26 December 1964

The snowfall, which began as a delightful gentle sprinkle on the evening of Christmas Day, confirming the immortal image of a White Christmas, had turned the Kurfürstendamm the following morning into a dismal scene. This was no longer the boulevard down which one would take pleasure in sauntering, for some days to come. However, unlike in the UK on the day after Christmas, trains and buses were running normally.

Unter den Linden, East Berlin, 26 December 1964
This looks westwards towards the Brandenburger Tor from the approximate location of the present-day Hotel Adlon. The pre-war Adlon was one of the great hotels of Europe, but was largely destroyed in 1945. At the time of this photograph the remains of the hotel, still functioning, lay off-camera to the left of the pillar clock, and the edifice was so near to the Berlin Wall that the windows on the western side were heavily festooned with metal bars. I had a drink there, and the term 'seen better days' came to mind. Otto-Grotewohl-Strasse was named after the first East German Prime Minister, who died three months before this photograph was taken.

Staatsoper, Unter den Linden, East Berlin, 26 December 1964
The Staatsoper (State Opera) Building, capacity 1,300, originates from the 1740s and after several reconstructions was finally rebuilt after extensive damage in the Second World War, and was reopened in 1955. It has a long history of hosting illustrious performances. The Operncafe, seen advertised here, later opened in a different location, but later closed permanently. The Staatsoper, also known as Lindenoper, still functions as a concert hall.

Karl-Marx-Allee, East Berlin, 26 December 1964, and Bernauer Strasse, West Berlin, 27 December 1964

The Berlin Wall divided families, and children on both sides grew up playing with their Christmas presents, never daring to believe that they would ever see their relatives who may be living a stone's throw away. It would be another twenty-five years before they were reunited.

Berlin Wall at Bernauer Strasse, 27 December 1964
If any picture symbolises the Cold War, surely this must be it. I took this photograph at Bernauer Strasse, the street where the windows of the buildings in East Berlin had been bricked up to foil escapes (as on the extreme right), the immediately adjoining pavement being in West Berlin. The graffito 'KZ' denotes *'Konzentrationslager'* (concentration camp). Also note two opposing propaganda boards, one Eastern and one Western, facing each other.

Eberswalder Strasse, East Berlin from Bernauer Strasse (West Berlin), 27 December 1964
The East German notice depicts people in West Berlin looking over the wall and then asks *'Warum so unbequem?'* ('Why so uncomfortable?'), and continues (in translation): 'You see more, you experience the truth; you can more objectively report, if you visit the capital of the German Democratic Republic, Berlin, yourself!'

Bernauer Strasse, Berlin, 27 December 1964
This shows a broad section of how the Berlin Wall had progressed in 1964 from the crude blocks that characterised it in its early years. Later it would become much higher. This is Bernauer Strasse, the street in which windows were bricked up to prevent escapes. The graffiti 'KZ' translate as 'concentration camp'. The term *'Trotz'* is an expression of defiance.

Bernauer Strasse at Brunnenstrasse, Berlin, 27 December 1964
This is the same location as photographed on page 65 and gives an interesting example of how the Berlin Wall evolved from crude concrete blocks to a more sophisticated design over the two years since that photograph. In later years the Wall was made considerably taller and was topped by a horizontal pole structure to prevent its being climbed, if indeed one could negotiate the wide control zone maintained by the East on the far side.

The road to Steinstücken, Berlin, 27 December 1964

Steinstücken was an exclave of West Berlin territory in the Zehlendorf area of south-west Berlin, and joined to the principal West Berlin area by a strip of disputed territory. In 1951 the East German Government attempted to annex the area, and the anomaly which existed here was the subject of much friction between East and West for many years. The situation was exacerbated by the existence of the East German rail line, which was positioned underneath Western or disputed territory.

Zonal border near Steinstücken, West Berlin, 27 December 1964

I spotted this board in a forest on the outer border of West Berlin, adjoining East Germany proper. Although at first glance this appears to be just another border warning notice, it was highly unusual to see as late as 1964 a reference to the 'Soviet Border'. East Germany, of course, maintained the pretence that it was a sovereign state over which the USSR had no control. In truth, of course, the DDR was neither German nor democratic.

Potsdam, East Germany, 7 June 1966

Although a British Citizen could travel to East Berlin without special permission, visiting East Germany proper ('The Zone') was not allowed unless, for example, one was on a guided tour, where one was closely managed. This excursion to Potsdam, just outside Berlin, provided an opportunity to see the situation in East Germany proper. Here, a group, possibly mainly tourists from the tour, examine a news-stand, watched by a portrait of Lenin.

Klement-Gottwald-Strasse, Potsdam, East Germany, 7 June 1966
Klement Gottwald (1896–1953) was the General Secretary of the Communist Party of Czechoslovakia from 1929 until 1945, and was later Prime Minister and President of that country. This is now Brandenburger Strasse, Potsdam's main shopping street. In the distance is the St Peter and Paul Church.

Fashion in East Germany, Potsdam, 7 June 1966
This was the cutting edge of fashion in East Germany in 1966. The window displays mostly had a somewhat faded look, with wares poorly displayed and reminiscent of the shop windows of wartime Britain.